Ask Me Anything

—

300 Questions to Help You Talk With the Children in Your Life.

Patricia Faulkner M.A. L.C.P.C.

This book is dedicated to Blake and Taylor. Without them, this book would never have been published.

CONTENTS

INTRODUCTION

Do you often find yourself wanting to have a meaningful conversation with the children in your life, or the children you work with, but you aren't sure how to start? Perhaps you would like to know more about how they are feeling, what they do with their friends, or how they feel about their family and their home. Maybe you would like to get something in response to your questions rather than just a shrug or a blank stare. If so, then this is the book that can help to provide the answers to all your questions! And best of all, it can eliminate the stress and frustration of trying to communicate with young people who often have difficulty expressing their thoughts and feelings.

As a Licensed Mental Health Therapist with 40 years' experience in the field of Mental Health, I've developed this book for parents, teachers, school counselors, mental health therapists, child providers, or anyone who finds themselves trying to have a more productive conversation with the children in their life.

Give it a try by using some of the suggestions in this book or make up your own rules! The most important thing is to just relax and have fun!

HOW TO USE THIS BOOK

There are many different ways to use this book. There are some suggestions that you might want to try but the most important thing is for everyone to be comfortable in expressing themselves. NEVER use this book as a threat or a punishment! Do not argue or disagree with the child's answers. Simply listen! Always present this book as something fun that you can do together.

SUGGESTIONS FOR USE

There are 300 questions in this book. Have the child call out a number between 1 and 300 and that is the question they can answer.

Take turns! Let the child ask you for a number and you answer a question as well, or else you can both answer the same question.

This book is divided into 8 parts: Myself, Home and Family, Friends, Physical Health, Emotions, Holidays and Celebrations, Just for Fun, and Bonus Questions. You might want to focus on a specific section. This can be especially helpful for teachers, school counselors or mental health professionals who are particularly interested in a certain part of the child's life.

If you are working with more than one child at a time, you might want to let them ask each other the questions while you just sit back and listen.

This book is great for therapy or counseling appointments, classroom relaxation time, or for fun family time. You can ask 1 question or 100. Do what works best for you and the child.

Consider keeping a notebook with the date and the responses in it. Later on, when the same question is asked again, you can go to the notebook and compare the answers.

Have fun and see what all you can learn!

SECTION ONE

MYSELF

1. What are 3 words that describe you?

2. What is something you would like to change about yourself?

3. What do you like best about yourself?

4. What is something you are really good at doing?

5. What is something you wish you could do better?

6. What is something you would like to tell me about yourself?

7. What dream do you remember from last night?

8. What would you like to do when you grow up?

9. What is scary to you about growing up?

10. What is exciting to you about growing up?

11. Do you think you will have children when you grow up?

12. Where would you like to live when you grow up?

13. What is your best memory from when you were younger?

14. What is something sad that has

happened to you?

15. What is your idea of the perfect day?

16. What do you wish you were doing

right now?

17. What feeling are you feeling right

now?

18. What question do you wish was in

this book?

19. Do you think you are mostly happy, mostly sad, mostly worried, or something else?

20. How do you think other people would describe you?

SECTION TWO

HOME AND FAMILY

21. Who in the family makes you laugh
    the most?

22. What family vacation was your
    favorite?

23. Do you like when the family eats meals together?

24. What do you wish was different about your house?

25. Does everyone in the family have chores they have to do?

26. With who in the family would you like to take a walk or a bike ride?

27. If you could plan a vacation for the family, where would you go?

28. Do you think your family argues a
     lot?

29. If you could plan a family dinner,
     what would you have?

30. What TV show does everyone in your
     family watch?

31. Do you think your family talks to
     each other very much?

32. If you could plan a family fun night,
     what would you plan?

33. Does anyone in the family like to play practical jokes?

34. Who is your favorite neighbor?

35. What is your favorite room in your house?

36. Is there anything you would like to change about your bedroom?

37. What do you like the most about the living room?

38. Do you have enough privacy in your house?

39. What is your least favorite room in your house?

40. Would you ever want to move to a new house? Why or why not?

41. What do you like to do with your grandparents?

42. What does your family fight about the most?

43. What do you like the best about the town where you live?

44. What is the worst thing about the town where you live?

45. Do you ever wish you had more brothers or sisters?

46. Is there anything you would like to change about the clothes in your closet?

47. Do you think your family spends enough time together?

48. What do you like best about your yard?

49. Is there anything you would change about your yard?

50. Where do you like to do your homework?

51. Who is your favorite person who comes to your home to visit?

52. Who does the most housework at your house?

53. Who does the most yard work at your house?

54. Do you wish you had a twin brother or sister?

55. What would you like to learn how to cook?

56. Do you wish something in your house could get fixed?

57. What is your favorite meal to have at home?

58. Is there something in your house that makes it hard for you to do your homework?

59. If you could paint your bedroom a different color, what color would you choose?

60. If you could do the grocery shopping by yourself, what groceries would you get for the week?

61. Do you like for your friends to come to your house? Why or why not?

62. What is something your family enjoys doing together?

63. What do you wish your family did more often?

64. What is something your family does together that you don't like?

65. Do you have cousins that you like to have around?

66. Are there any aunts or uncles you wish you could see more often?

67. Is there anyone in your family who has died? Did you know them very well?

68. What do you think is the very best

thing about your family?

SECTION THREE

FRIENDS

69. What friend have you known the
    longest?

70. What is your favorite thing to do with
    your friends?

71. Who are your best friends?

72. When was the last time you had a fight with one of your friends?

73. Do you and your friends like the same shows on TV?

74. Where do you and your friends like to eat?

75. Are you in any clubs or groups with your friends?

76. Do any of your friends play musical
     instruments?

77. Have any of your friends ever
     smoked or drank alcohol?

78. What time do your friends usually go
     to bed?

79. What friend do you argue with the
     most?

80. What friend's house do you like to
     visit the most?

81. What was the last fun thing you did with one of your friends?

82. Is there anyone who you wish was your friend?

83. If you could take your friends anywhere on a vacation, where would you take them?

84. Who is your smartest friend?

85. Do any of your friends have chores they have to do?

86. What makes you and your friends laugh?

87. Do you have a friend who is sad a lot of the time?

88. What do your friends like the best about you?

89. With which friend do you have the most fun?

90. If you and your friends could go to any restaurant, where would you go?

91. Which friend do you go to the most when you need help?

92. Which of your friends complains the most?

93. Do any of your friends get in trouble at school?

94. If you made a movie about you and your friends, what would you call it?

95. Do you and your friends like the same kind of music?

96. If money was no problem, what gift would you like to give to your friends?

97. What is your favorite thing to talk about with your friends?

98. If you could turn yourself and your friends into animals for one day, which animals would you choose?

99. If you and your friends had your own TV show, what would it be about?

100. If you could switch houses with one of your friends, whose house would you pick?

101. What is something that is done at one

of your friends' house that you wish

could be done at your house?

102. When was the last time you helped one

of your friends?

103. What do you wish you could change

about your group of friends?

104. What was the last thing that made you

and your friends very sad?

105. Is there someone in school that you wish was your friend?

106. What do you and your friends talk about the most?

107. What is your least favorite thing to do with your friends?

108. What was the last thing that made you and your friends very happy?

109. What do you and your friends argue about the most?

110. If you could pick any famous person to be your friend, who would you pick and what would you do with them?

SECTION FOUR

PHYSICAL HEALTH

111. What is your favorite exercise?

112. What is something about your body

you would change if you could?

113. What sport do you wish you could play?

114. How much water do you drink every day?

115. How many jumping jacks can you do?

116. If you could be in charge of a P.E. or exercise class for a day, what would you have everyone do?

117. What do you like best about your body?

118. What is something you do every day that is good for you?

119. Do you eat a healthy breakfast?

120. Do you think you eat too much, too little, or just about the right amount?

121. What is your favorite vegetable?

122. How well do you sleep at night?

123. Do you have too much or too little energy?

124. How long do you think you could go with no junk food at all?

125. What kinds of fruit do you like?

126. What do you do when you can't fall asleep?

127. Do you get a lot of headaches? If so, when do you usually get them?

128. When was the last time you went to see the Doctor?

129. Do you have any problems going to the bathroom?

130. How often do you wake up during the night?

131. Are you having any physical pain right now?

132. Are you as strong as you want to be?

133. What sports do you like to play?

134. Do you get a lot of stomach aches? If yes, when do you usually get them?

135. How far do you think you could run without taking a break?

SECTION FIVE

EMOTIONS

136. What makes you happy?

137. Who do you like to spend time with when you're sad?

138. Do you ever feel lonely? When?

139. When do you get the most frustrated?

140. Do you have trouble paying attention? When?

141. Have you ever had thoughts of wanting to hurt yourself?

142. What is something that makes you want to scream?

143. What are 3 things that you are afraid of?

144. When you're having a bad day, what
can I do to make it better?

145. What do you worry about the most?

146. How do you feel about what you see on
the news?

147. How are you feeling right this minute?

148. What makes you feel excited?

149. Do your feelings change a lot during
the day?

150. When was the last time you felt sad?

151. When do you get bored?

152. What kinds of things make you angry?

153. When you're sad, what do you do to feel

better?

154. Who do you know who always seems

to be happy?

155. Do you keep a diary or a journal? If not, would you like to start?

156. What do you do to calm down when you are angry?

157. Who do you know who always seems sad?

158. Is there anything you feel guilty about?

159. What makes you feel jealous?

160. What do you like about yourself?

161. Who do you know who always seems

angry?

162. What is something that makes you

laugh?

163. What is something that makes you cry?

SECTION SIX

HOLIDAYS AND
CELEBRATIONS

164. Do you make New Year's Resolutions?

165. What do you like best about Valentine's

Day?

166. What would you do if you were in

charge of planning an Easter Egg Hunt?

167. If you could fill up an Easter egg basket

for your family, what would you put in

it?

168. If you could fill up an Easter egg basket

for your friends, what would you put in

it?

169. What is your favorite thing about your

birthday?

170. Do you like to go to birthday parties?

171. Who would you like to come to your birthday party?

172. What would you like to have to eat for your birthday this year?

173. If you had no money, what could you give someone for their birthday?

174. What is one of the best birthday gifts you've ever received?

175. What do you wish you could give to someone in your family for their birthday this year?

176. What does your family do on the 4th of July?

177. What is your favorite thing about the 4th of July?

178. What do you like about parades?

179. Have you ever been in a parade? If not, would you like to be in one?

180. Do you like to dress up for Halloween?

181. If you could be anybody or anything for Halloween, who or what would you be?

182. If you could throw a Halloween party, what would you do and who would you invite?

183. What is your favorite Halloween candy?

184. If you could pick out costumes for your mom or dad to wear on Halloween, what costumes would you choose?

185. What do you like best about Thanksgiving?

186. Does your family say what they are most thankful for on Thanksgiving? What are you most thankful for this year?

187. What kind of meal would you like for Thanksgiving this year?

188. What is your favorite Thanksgiving Day tradition?

189. What Christmas decoration is your favorite?

190. Do you like decorating for Christmas?

191. What kind of Christmas decorations have you made yourself? Would you like to make more this year?

192. Does your family have any Christmas traditions? If so, which ones are your favorite?

193. Is there anything you don't like about Christmas?

194. Do you ever make presents for others? Would you like to make some this year?

195. What is your favorite Christmas carol?

196. Is there anything different you'd like to do this Christmas?

197. What are your favorite Christmas foods? If you could plan Christmas this year, what would you be sure to do?

198. What do you hope to get for Christmas this year?

199. Do you celebrate New Year's Eve? If so, how do you celebrate?

200. If you could plan a New Year's Eve party, who would you invite and what would you do? What would you have for your guests to eat?

201. What is your favorite thing about New Year's Eve?

SECTION SEVEN

SCHOOL

202. Besides recess, what is your favorite

thing about school?

203. Who is the best teacher you've ever

had?

204. What is something you are learning in school right now?

205. What classes in school do you like the best?

206. If you could make up a school class, what would it be?

207. What subject in school would you most like to teach?

208. What do you think is the biggest problem in your school?

209. Who do you go to if you are having a problem in school?

210. What are your least favorite classes in school?

211. Are your friends in your classes at school?

212. When is the best time for you to do your homework?

213. Where is the best place for you to do your homework?

214. Is there anyone who you like to help you with your homework?

215. Are there any clubs or activities or sports at school that you would like to try?

216. How do the kids act in the hallways at your school?

217. Are you ever afraid when you are at school? If so, when is that?

218. Who do you usually sit with for lunch at school?

219. What is your favorite school lunch?

220. What is in your desk or locker at school?

221. What is your least favorite school lunch?

222. How would you describe the teacher(s) you have this year?

223. Do you wish your school was larger, smaller, or just the size it is?

224. If you could plan the lunch for school one day, what would you serve?

225. What do you wish your school had that they currently don't have?

226. If you could pick the hours for your school, when would it start and when would it end?

227. Are there any bullies at your school? If so, what does the school do about them?

228. Who do you like the best in your whole school?

229. If you could decorate your school room however you wanted, what would it look like?

230. Is there anyone in your school that scares you?

231. Who is the nicest person to you at your
    school?

232. What would you change about your
    class if you were the teacher?

233. What would you change about the
    school if you were the principal?

234. Are there different groups of kids at
    your school? (Popular kids, jocks, etc.)

SECTION EIGHT

JUST FOR FUN

235. If you could have a whole day to do whatever you wanted to do, what would you do and who would be with you?

236. What is your favorite ride at a carnival or amusement park?

237. If you could visit anywhere in the world for 1 week, where would you go?

238. What color of hair would you like to have for one month?

239. What would you like to be famous for doing?

240. If you could only eat 3 things for 1 year, what would you eat?

241. What do you hope is different in 1
year?

242. What is something you have always
wanted to try?

243. If you could take a field trip and learn
about anything, where would you go?

244. How would you communicate with
others if you couldn't talk or use your
phone for a whole week?

245. What is your favorite song?

246. On a scale of 1 – 10, how much do you like playing video games? Which one is your favorite?

247. What is your favorite way to get a hold of your friends when you want to talk to them?

248. Who is your favorite person in the entire world and why are they your favorite?

249. If you could study one subject all day long, what would you study?

250. Who do you admire the most?

251. On a scale of 1 – 10, how important is social media to you?

252. What are your 3 favorite things to do?

253. If you could be any animal in the world, what animal would you be and how long would you choose to be this animal?

254. What 2 colors do you think go the best together?

255. What is something you wish you knew more about?

256. If all of your clothes had to be just one color, which color would you choose?

257. What is your favorite form of social media?

258. If you could be invisible for 1 day, what would you do?

259. If you could be any superhero for 1 week, who would you be and what would you do?

260. What is something you wish you knew about your mom and dad?

261. If you were given $100 to spend at your favorite store, what would you buy?

262. What movie that you've seen would you like for them to remake with you as the star?

263. If you were given the power to fly for just 1 day, where would you go?

264. What is the funniest joke you know?

265. What is something you would do for 1 million dollars that you wouldn't normally do?

266. When do you most like to be given a hug?

267. What has been the best year of your life so far?

268. If you could own any type of business,
     what type of business would you choose
     to own?

269. If you could change any one thing
     about the world, what would you
     change?

270. What is something about yourself that
     you really wish your family knew?

SECTION NINE

BONUS QUESTIONS

271. If someone gave you $1,000, what would you do with it?

272. If you could have anything you wanted tonight for supper, what would you have?

273. What is your least favorite color?

274. If you could take your family anywhere on vacation, where would you take them?

275. If you could change one thing about your home, what would you change?

276. Is there somebody who has died who you still really miss?

277. If you had to eat only 1 food for an entire week, what would it be?

278. What is the worst smell?

279. What is the worst thing about going to the doctor?

280. What is your favorite sport to watch?

281. Do you pray?

282. What is your favorite thing to do for exercise?

283. What helps you the most when you are feeling stressed?

284. If someone gave you the opportunity to see 5 years into the future, would you look?

285. If you could go back and change 1 thing about your life, what would you change?

286. What is your favorite store?

287. Where is your favorite place to eat?

288. If you had the chance to go back and live this past year again, would you do it?

289. What is the most children you think anyone should have?

290. What do you think will be different about your life in 10 years?

291. Do you think it's ok to keep secrets?

292. What has been your favorite age so far?

293. Do you ever wish there were more

children in your family?

294. How can I best help you when you are

having a bad day?

295. How do you know when your mom or

dad is happy?

296. What is your favorite thing about the

room we're in right now?

297. What has been the best thing about

today?

298. What has been the worst thing about today?

299. What is your favorite season?

300. If you could, would you start today over again? Why or why not?